A star-forming region called the Pillars of Creation

Conditions in the Tarantula Nebula show scientists what our own Milky Way galaxy was like billions of years ago, when stars were forming at an extremely fast pace.

NATIONAL GEOGRAPHIC KiDS

BEYOND INFINITY

EXPLORING THE SECRETS OF THE UNIVERSE WITH THE JAMES WEBB SPACE TELESCOPE

STEPHANIE WARREN DRIMMER

NATIONAL GEOGRAPHIC
WASHINGTON, D.C.

The spiral galaxy pictured here, NGC 1300, measures about 59,000 light-years across. That means it would take 59,000 years to go from one side to the other, traveling at the speed of light!

TABLE OF CONTENTS

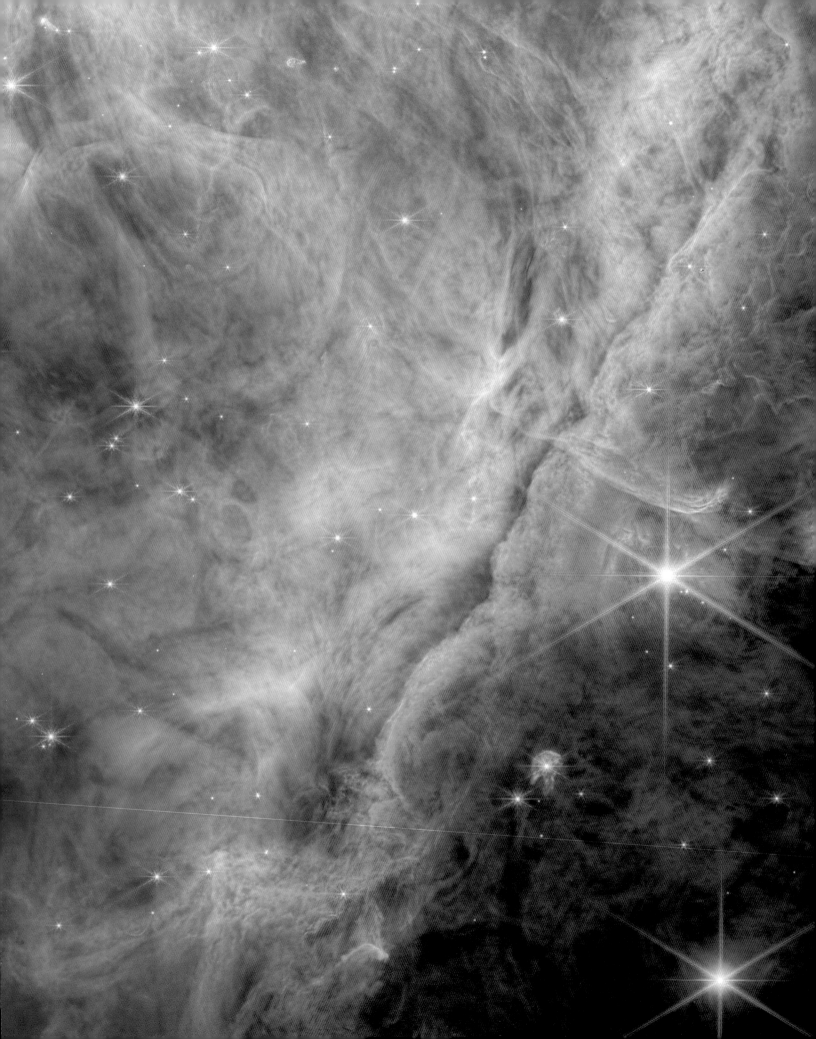

From detecting carbon—the molecule that makes life on Earth possible—in the Orion Nebula (left), to observing newborn stars (above), the James Webb Space Telescope is giving scientists a brand-new look at our universe.

1
SEEING
INTO THE PAST

IMAGINE HITTING REWIND ON THE HISTORY OF THE UNIVERSE.

Before your eyes, skyscrapers shrink. Roads retreat and disappear. The Egyptian pyramids sink down into the sand.

Then, in a blip, humans are gone. Dinosaurs rise up from the dead and rule again, then vanish. The continents come together. The oceans dry up. Earth becomes a ball of hot magma.

Then Earth disappears entirely. Along with other planets, it dissolves into pebbles, then dust. As you watch, the whole universe shrinks, all that dust and gas pulling inward. One by one, stars blink out. At the end, there is nothing left.

Many people have dreamed of time machines able to transport them to the past. But we already have time machines. We just call them telescopes.

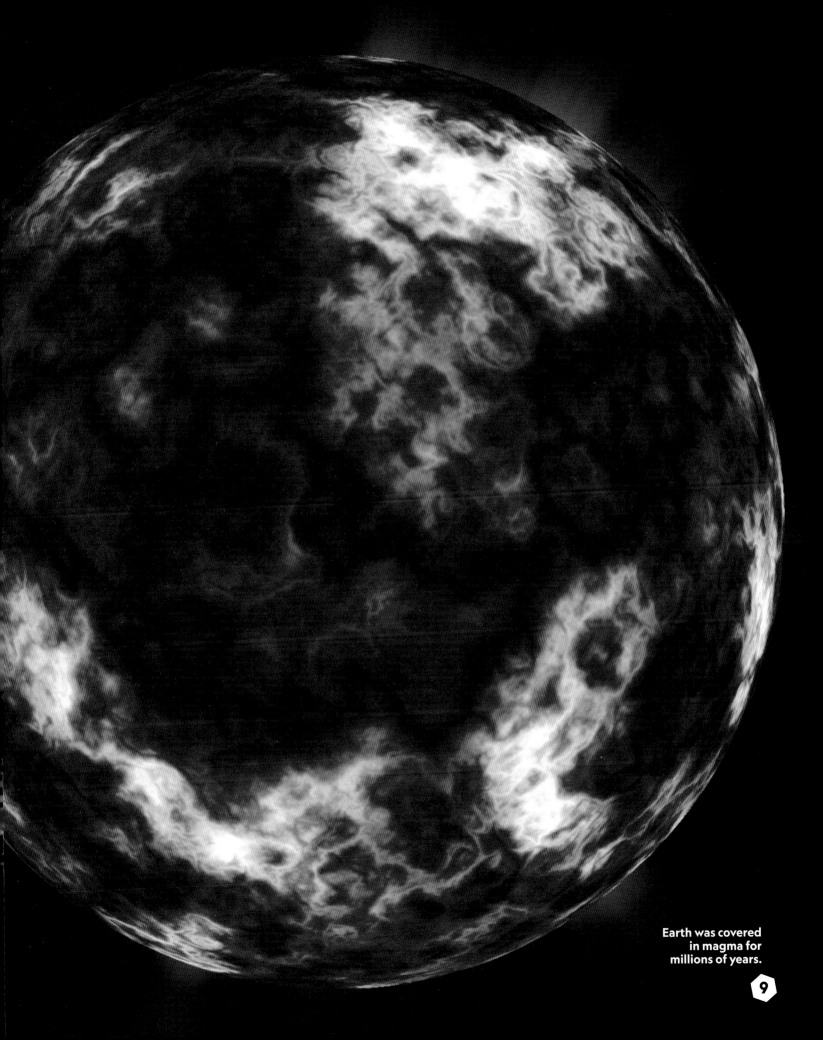

Earth was covered
in magma for
millions of years.

9

TELESCOPE OR TIME MACHINE?

Telescopes see light from distant objects, like galaxies, stars, and planets. And although light travels fast (after all, it's the fastest thing in the universe!), these objects are so far away that it can take years for light to travel through space to the lenses of our telescopes. So when we observe distant objects, we are seeing them as they looked in the past, not as they appear today.

LOOKING BACK

The farther into space we look, the further back in time we are looking, too. Light reflecting off Jupiter takes about 43 minutes to reach us. So a telescope on Earth that's focused on Jupiter sees it as it was 43 minutes earlier. Point your telescope at Proxima Centauri, the nearest star to our sun, and you'll see it as it was about four years earlier. View Polaris, the North Star, and you're looking 320 years into the past.

QUESTIONS AND ANSWERS

Scientists have long wanted to peer at the very farthest reaches of space, because these super-distant stars and galaxies would appear as they were more than 13 billion years ago, when the universe was just forming. That would help researchers answer the biggest question in astronomy: How did everything begin? But they didn't have a telescope that could see that far back in time ... until the launch of the James Webb Space Telescope. It is the most powerful telescope in history. And it's already answering some of the biggest questions in astronomy, from "How are stars born?" to "Could life exist on other planets?"

HOW FAR BACK IN TIME WILL THE JAMES WEBB SPACE TELESCOPE SEE?

PRESENT DAY

4.6 billion
years ago
**OUR SUN
FORMS**

13 billion to
10 billion
years ago
**MANY QUASARS*
FORM**

More than
13 billion
+
years ago
**FIRST GALAXIES
FORM**

About
13.8 billion
years ago
BIG BANG

*Quasars are extremely bright
celestial objects. They are thought to
be powered by supermassive black
holes at the center of some galaxies.

3 ... 2 ... 1 ...
BLASTOFF!

Astronomers around the world didn't get much sleep on December 24, 2021. On that Christmas Eve, they were hoping for an extra-special holiday gift the next morning: the smooth launch of the telescope they had spent more than 25 years designing, building, and testing.

LAUNCH DAY

Things were especially tense at ELA-3, the launchpad located in French Guiana where the rocket carrying the telescope would take off. The launch had already been delayed for weeks as the rainy season kept conditions too dangerous. Finally, the team got a window of clear weather that Christmas morning. The control room filled with anxious scientists. At last, it was time.

At 7:20 a.m. on December 25, 2021, a voice counted down from 10 in French, and the Ariane 5 rocket—with its precious cargo folded inside—lurched on the launchpad. Riding a column of smoke and fire, it rose into the sky. "Go, Webb!" shouted operations manager Jean-Luc Voyer. Scientists cheered, clapped, and hugged.

The launch was the most dangerous part of the mission, because if something went wrong, scientists could do nothing but watch as the rocket turned into a fireball. But once it cleared Earth's atmosphere and entered outer space, the James Webb Space Telescope— JWST for short—was just getting started.

EARTH'S SPIN HELPED GIVE JWST AN EXTRA PUSH DURING ITS LAUNCH.

JWST
separating
from Ariane 5
rocket

ALL SYSTEMS GO

After exiting the atmosphere, the telescope began what many called its "two weeks of terror": a series of steps to unfold the giant device and get it working. Scientists had practiced this over and over. But there's nothing like doing it for real, on a rocket traveling at about 700 miles an hour (1,127 km/h).

First, the telescope had to separate from the rocket. Then it booted up its solar panel to get power. Small rockets fired to correct its course. Then came the hard part: For the next two weeks, its sunshield unfolded in a series of precise movements. All in all, 344 things had to go exactly right. Amazingly, they did. On January 8, 2022, the giant gold flower of JWST's mirror pointed toward the distant universe, ready to see things that had never been seen before.

Ariane 5
rocket launch

AN EYE IN THE SKY

Building and launching a game-changing telescope was no small feat. It took decades, the work of thousands of scientists and engineers, and cooperation across 14 countries. But the result was worth the effort: JWST is six times larger and 100 times more powerful than the last record-breaking telescope, the Hubble Space Telescope.

SEEING RED

Most telescopes are just mightier versions of our eyes: They mostly detect what's called visible light, the type of light we can see. But visible light is only a small part of the entire light spectrum. With JWST, scientists wanted to take a look at a type of light that's invisible to us, called infrared. Though we can't see infrared, we can feel it as heat. The light from the very first stars and galaxies that ever formed—the most distant objects in the universe—is infrared. That's because as light travels great distances it gets stretched out to longer wavelengths into the infrared part of the light spectrum (see diagram below). JWST's infrared eyes will bring these once invisible stars and galaxies into view.

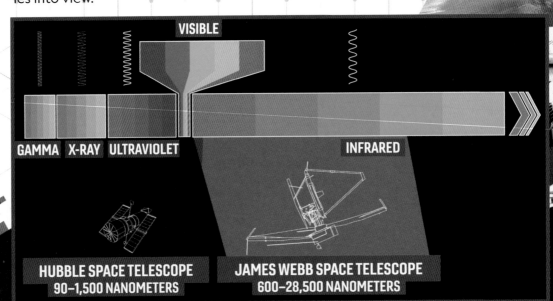

GAMMA   X-RAY   ULTRAVIOLET   VISIBLE   INFRARED

HUBBLE SPACE TELESCOPE	JAMES WEBB SPACE TELESCOPE
90–1,500 NANOMETERS	600–28,500 NANOMETERS

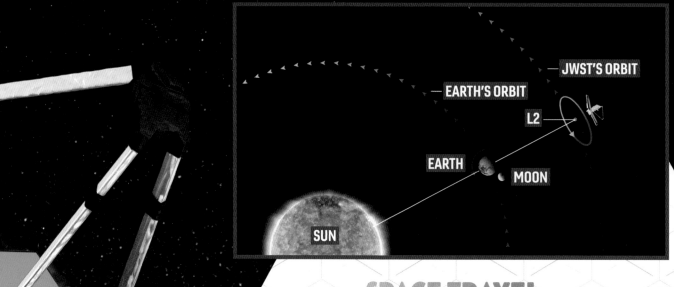

JWST'S ORBIT

EARTH'S ORBIT

L2

EARTH

MOON

SUN

SPACE TRAVEL

There's one big problem with a telescope that sees heat: There are a lot of hot things in space! Heat from much closer, larger space objects, like Earth and the sun, overpowers the faint heat coming from distant stars and galaxies. To allow JWST to do its job, scientists had to get it away from these closer objects. So scientists positioned JWST about a million miles (1.6 million km) away from Earth, in a special spot in space called the second Lagrange point, or L2. There, gravity from Earth and the sun pull on JWST just the right amount to keep it positioned behind Earth, which blocks the sun's heat and light. Once in position, JWST uses its giant sunshield to block even more heat.

JWST OPERATES AT
**MINUS 370°
FAHRENHEIT**
(-223° CELSIUS).
BRRR!

WHAT'S ON BOARD

How does the most sophisticated telescope in history work? JWST collects light from a star, planet, or other space object with its large main mirror. The main mirror reflects and focuses the light into a smaller, secondary mirror, which then directs that light into one or more of JWST's four scientific instruments. Meanwhile, the telescope's enormous sunshield protects the sensitive instruments from heat and light. At the same time, the solar array captures sunlight for power.

SCIENCE INSTRUMENT MODULE
This houses JWST's "brain": its cameras and scientific instruments.

SOLAR PANELS
These take in sunlight and convert it to electricity to power JWST.

TELESCOPE ORIGAMI
JWST's main mirror is so large that in order to fit inside a rocket, it had to be folded up like origami. Once in space, it had to unfold by itself.

ANTENNA
The antenna receives instructions from Earth and beams back information.

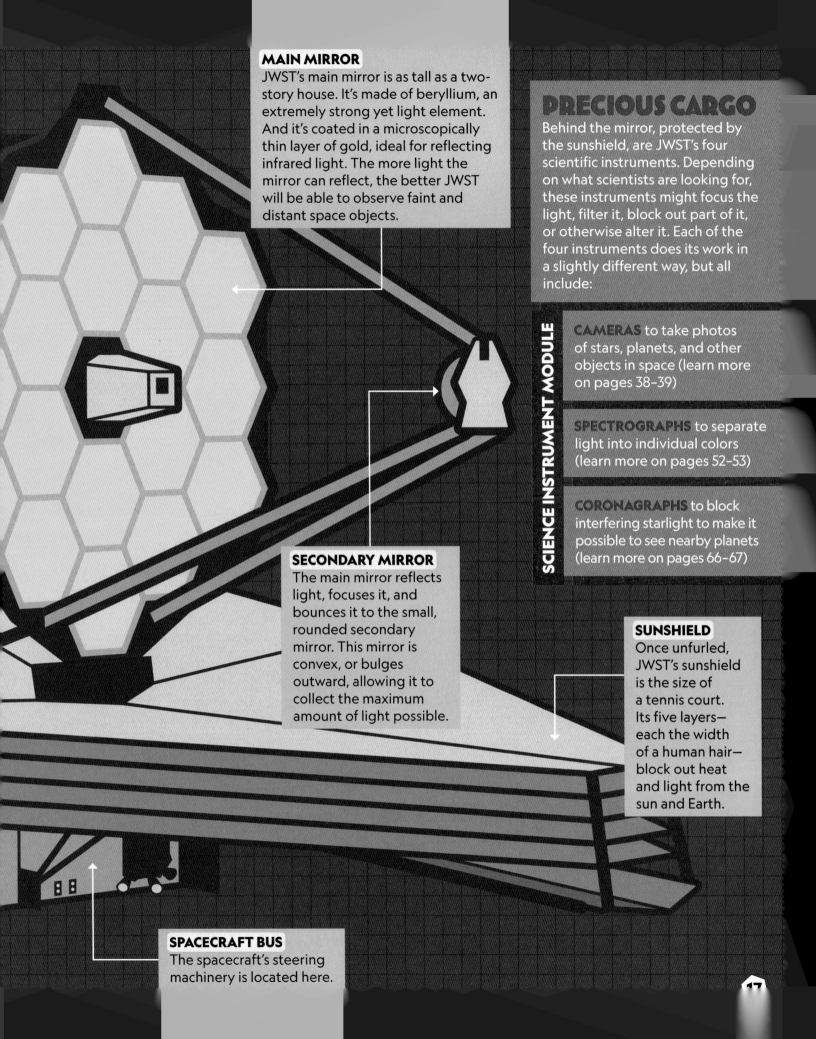

MAIN MIRROR
JWST's main mirror is as tall as a two-story house. It's made of beryllium, an extremely strong yet light element. And it's coated in a microscopically thin layer of gold, ideal for reflecting infrared light. The more light the mirror can reflect, the better JWST will be able to observe faint and distant space objects.

PRECIOUS CARGO
Behind the mirror, protected by the sunshield, are JWST's four scientific instruments. Depending on what scientists are looking for, these instruments might focus the light, filter it, block out part of it, or otherwise alter it. Each of the four instruments does its work in a slightly different way, but all include:

SCIENCE INSTRUMENT MODULE

CAMERAS to take photos of stars, planets, and other objects in space (learn more on pages 38–39)

SPECTROGRAPHS to separate light into individual colors (learn more on pages 52–53)

CORONAGRAPHS to block interfering starlight to make it possible to see nearby planets (learn more on pages 66–67)

SECONDARY MIRROR
The main mirror reflects light, focuses it, and bounces it to the small, rounded secondary mirror. This mirror is convex, or bulges outward, allowing it to collect the maximum amount of light possible.

SUNSHIELD
Once unfurled, JWST's sunshield is the size of a tennis court. Its five layers—each the width of a human hair—block out heat and light from the sun and Earth.

SPACECRAFT BUS
The spacecraft's steering machinery is located here.

HUBBLE VS. JWST

JWST isn't just peering at unstudied regions of space. It's also taking a new look at all kinds of space objects that its predecessor, the Hubble Space Telescope, also captured. JWST's infrared vision is already revealing hidden secrets about galaxies, nebulas ... and even planets in our own solar system.

HUBBLE TELESCOPE

JAMES WEBB SPACE TELESCOPE

SEEING STARS

One of JWST's best tricks is its ability to see through gas and dust to peek at what's lurking behind it. Here, it's peering through part of the Carina Nebula to see glittering stars in the process of being born.

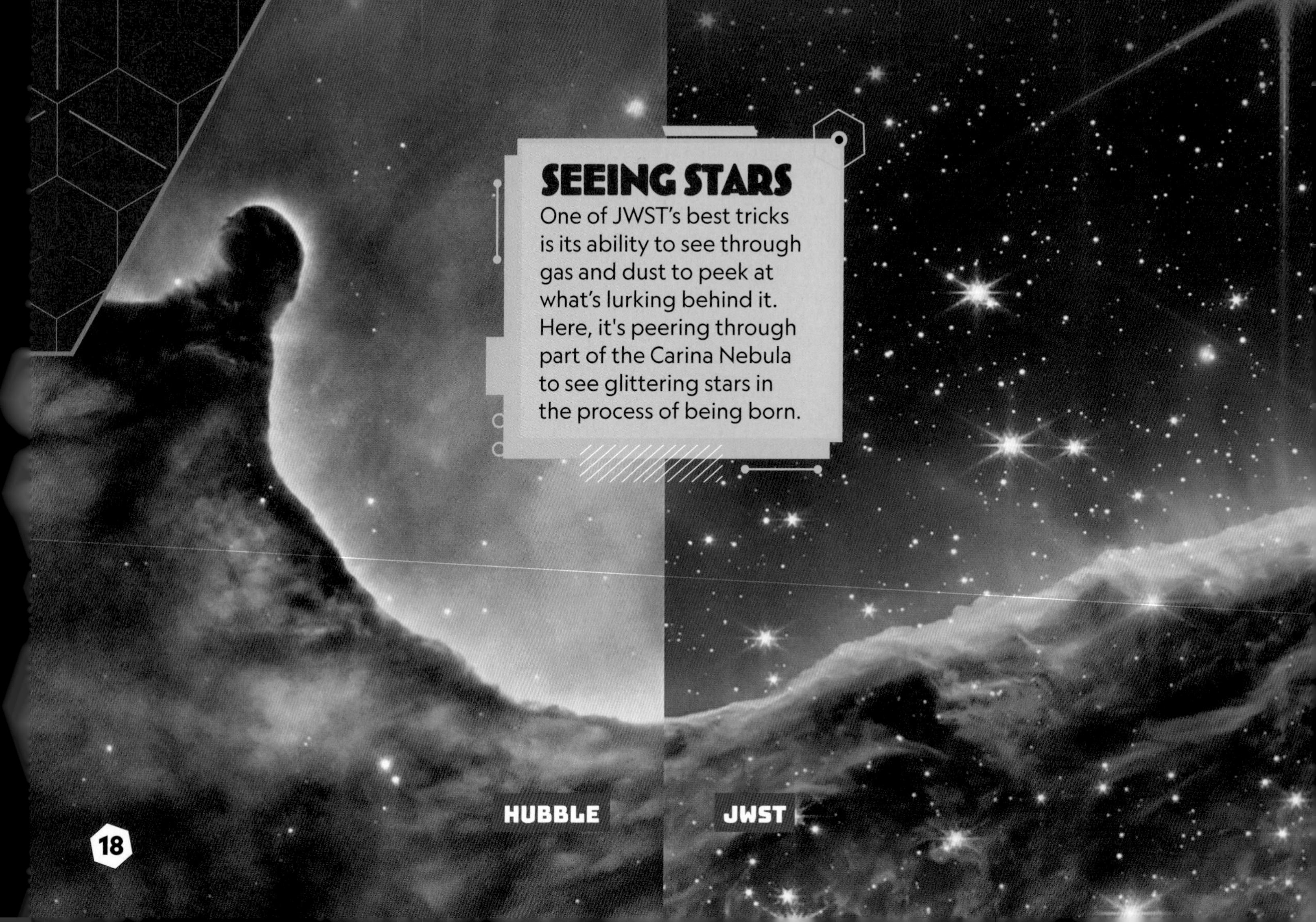

HUBBLE

JWST

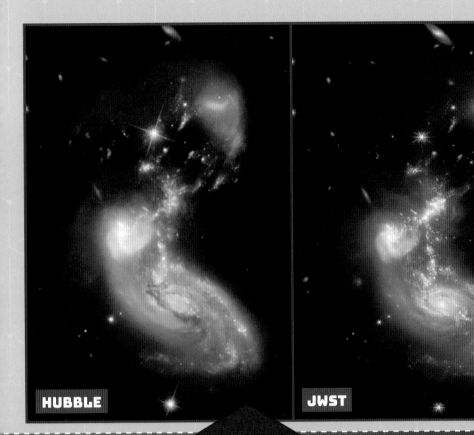

HUBBLE

JWST

GALACTIC BALLET

What happens when two galaxies collide? Just ask JWST! These two galaxies, located about 500 million light-years from Earth, are in the process of merging. As they come together, the pull of their gravitational fields is twisting and distorting their shapes.

UNLIKE JWST, **HUBBLE ORBITS EARTH,** TRAVELING AT A BLISTERING 17,000 MILES AN HOUR (27,400 KM/H).

HUBBLE

JWST

STELLAR PATTERNS

To JWST's infrared eyes, the spiral IC 5332 galaxy looks as intricate as a snowflake. The tangled pattern is made up of gases dotted with stars. IC 5332 is known for its position: It is almost perfectly aligned so that its spiral arms are visible from Earth.

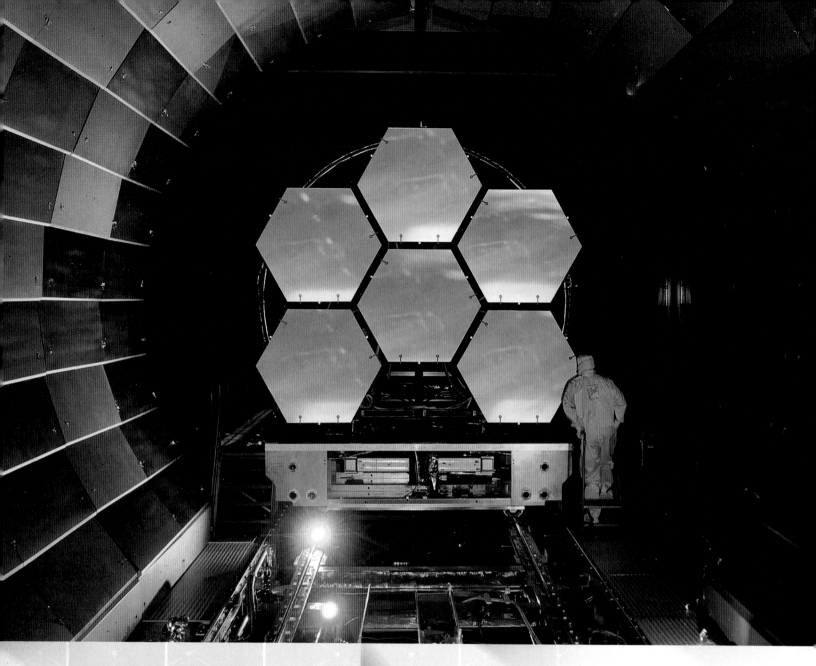

(Above) JWST's mirrors undergo testing to make sure they can stand up to the extremely cold temperatures of space.

(Right) The mirrors' gold coating is extremely reflective, especially of infrared light. This helps the telescope capture more light.

(Far right) Scientists once used this enormous chamber to test the toughness of the Apollo spacecraft that landed the first people on the moon. The chamber was updated to fit the JWST.

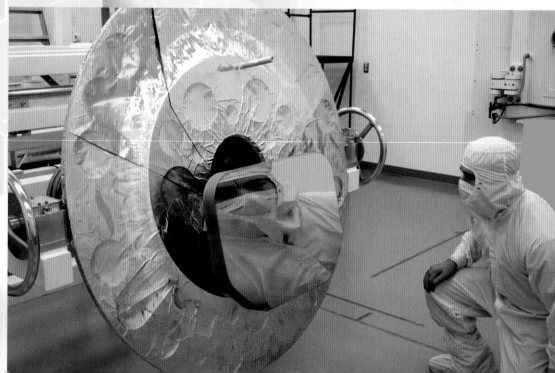

2
HOW DID THE UNIVERSE BEGIN?

THE UNIVERSE IS DOTTED WITH COUNTLESS GALAXIES.

They are beautiful: shaped like spirals, disks, and clouds, sparkling with stars. But when the universe first banged into existence, there were no galaxies. Instead, space was filled with a hot soup of particles (tiny specks of matter). How did that smooth pool of stuff become stars, plants, comets, us—everything that fills space today?

To answer that question, scientists need to peer at the very oldest galaxies—the first to be born. Enter the JWST. Its infrared sensors are giving astronomers a whole new view of galaxies like the Cartwheel galaxy, the large wheel-shaped one pictured here. That's helping scientists paint a picture of the beginning of ... well, everything.

The Cartwheel galaxy was born when a large spiral galaxy crashed into a smaller galaxy.

GROWING UP GALAXY

t took a very long time for light from galaxy JADES-GS-z13-0 to reach JWST's giant gold mirrors: more than 13 billion years! That means images from the telescope show this galaxy as it looked when it was first born, soon after the formation of the universe about 13.8 billion years ago. It's one of the oldest galaxies we have ever observed—so far away that it looks faint even to superpowered JWST.

BANG!

The very farthest and oldest galaxies are more than cosmic curiosities. They are shaking up what we know about what the universe looked like at its birth, during what astronomers call the big bang. During this explosive event, all the matter that exists now expanded out of a single point. The newborn universe was a mix of superhot particles, energy, and light. Over time, the particles, called atoms, came together to form planets, stars, and eventually, the groups of stars called galaxies.

Images captured by the Hubble Space Telescope—JWST's older sibling—hinted that there might be a lot of these very early galaxies. But Hubble can only see so much. The most ancient galaxies are so far away that their light has stretched into infrared. To understand this, picture holding a Slinky between your hands. Light travels in waves, like the coils of a Slinky. Now picture pulling the two ends of the Slinky apart. That's what happens to light as it moves through the vastness of space: It gets stretched out. Eventually it stretches so much that it becomes a new type of light: infrared, the light JWST was designed to see.

UNSEEN UNIVERSE

On July 11, 2022, this large image of glittering galaxies became the first JWST photo revealed to the public. It displays the deep infrared universe. Before JWST, this chunk of sky looked dim. But the telescope revealed it was hiding never-before-seen galaxies: perhaps more than 19 of them!

So far, JWST is revealing that there are many more ancient galaxies in the universe than experts thought. That means that galaxies—and also the stars that they are made of—began to form from the particle soup of the growing universe very early on. Some astronomers think the first stars may have been born just about 200 million years after the big bang—when the universe was just an infant!

VISIBLE

INFRARED

With its ability to see infrared light, JWST can look through the thick dust clouds that make up this "star nursery" called the Carina Nebula. The reddish areas show the youngest stars, in the process of forming.

BUILDING THE
MIRROR AND SUNSHIELD

JWST's shiny gold mirror is as big as a house. Its enormous size is what makes the telescope so powerful. But there's a catch: The mirror is too big to fit in any rocket!

To make it fit, engineers had to design the mirror to fold up like origami. Then it had to unfold in space on its own, with no human help. And the unfolded mirror had to be perfectly smooth—no folds, creases, or bumps—to create clear images. It seemed like an impossible challenge. But JWST engineers made it happen.

MIRROR, MIRROR

Why would a telescope need a mirror anyway? Most early telescopes used pieces of curved glass to bend light and bring faraway objects into focus (just like eyeglasses). But modern large telescopes use curved mirrors instead. These mirrors gather and concentrate light. That allows them to capture light that is very faint, like the light coming from faraway galaxies or planets orbiting other suns.

JWST's house-size mirror is made up of 18 smaller mirrors that unfold into a honeycomb pattern. Extremely precise motors shift the mirrors into perfect position. The motors are able to move the mirrors incredibly tiny distances, tens of thousands of times smaller than the period at the end of this sentence.

JWST'S MIRRORS ARE SUPER REFLECTIVE, CAPTURING ABOUT 98 PERCENT OF INCOMING LIGHT.

SUN PROTECTION

In order to sense faint infrared signals coming from far away, JWST needs to block out the much greater heat coming from the sun, Earth, and moon. So engineers outfitted JWST with a sunshield the size of a tennis court. When unfolded, it acts like a giant beach umbrella, blocking light and cooling the telescope to minus 370°F (-223°C), the extremely low temperature that the telescope's instruments need to work. That's more than two times colder than the coldest spot in Antarctica!

In order to be light enough for the rocket to carry, JWST's sunshield had to be made of fabric. But fabric could easily snag or rip as it unfolded, which would make the telescope useless. Engineers decided to use a thin but extremely strong plastic material called Kapton. The sunshield has five layers, giving it plenty of backups in case something like a flying space rock tears a hole in the shade.

When JWST launched, its mirror and sunshield unfolded perfectly. Now they're working together: The sunshield protects the mirror from light and heat, allowing it to capture images from the oldest and most distant parts of the universe.

STEPHAN'S QUINTET

ABOUT 290 MILLION LIGHT-YEARS FROM EARTH, FOUR GALAXIES

TWIRL AND DANCE

AROUND EACH OTHER.

This group of galaxies is called Stephan's Quintet (though "quintet" means "five," only four of the galaxies are actually close together). The top galaxy in the image is home to an enormous black hole (a place in space where gravity is so strong that even light can't get out) ... and it's in a feeding frenzy. Stars, gas, and dust swirl around it, drawn into orbit by the black hole's enormous gravity. As it snacks on anything that gets too close, the black hole shoots out jets of particles traveling at light speed. Scientists now think that nearly all large galaxies—including our own Milky Way—have one of these "supermassive" black holes at their center. And JWST will help scientists figure out how these black holes feed and grow.

SOME
SUPERMASSIVE
BLACK HOLES
ARE A BILLION
TIMES MORE
MASSIVE THAN
OUR SUN.

SHAPING GALAXIES

Galaxies are where gravity holds together collections of gas, dust, and stars—a lot of stars. Big galaxies can contain 100 trillion of them! There are four main types of galaxies.

SPIRAL

Our own Milky Way is this type of galaxy, resembling a giant rotating pinwheel. The bulge in the middle is made up of many stars clustered tightly together. The arms are rich in gas, material for new stars to form.

IRREGULAR

Any galaxy with a strange shape—such as a toothpick or a ring—fits in this galaxy grab-bag category. Astronomers think these strange shapes occur when galaxies get close enough to one another for their gravitational pulls to have a warping effect.

ELLIPTICAL

These galaxies don't have much in the way of structure, and their stars—mostly older in age—orbit in random directions. Scientists think that elliptical galaxies occur when spiral galaxies collide and merge.

LENTICULAR

These galaxies are a bit like a cross between a spiral galaxy and an elliptical galaxy. Like a spiral galaxy, they have a central bulge. But like an elliptical galaxy, they are made up of older stars.

31

MEET QUYEN HART

Quyen Hart is an astronomer in charge of Webb science communication at the Space Telescope Science Institute in Baltimore, Maryland, U.S.A.

Q: WHAT CAN JWST TEACH US ABOUT THE BEGINNING OF THE UNIVERSE?

A: We know that it all started with the big bang. That's when the universe began as a single point that stretched and expanded to become as big as it is now. And it is still expanding! Near the beginning, the universe was dense, filled with hot matter and light. That light—the first light to travel through the universe—is called the cosmic microwave background radiation, and it's still moving through the universe. It's invisible to the human eye, but radio telescopes can pick it up. That's how we got a picture of the earliest universe.

We also know what the universe was like about 500 million years after the big bang: It was filled with galaxies. That's as far back as the Hubble Space Telescope is able to look. So before JWST came along, it was like astronomers had a book about the history of the universe that was missing pages. They had the introduction, but then the first chapter—what happened in the hundreds of millions of years after the big bang—was missing. JWST is filling in that blank chapter right now!

Rosette Nebula

Q: WHAT HAS IT DISCOVERED SO FAR?

A: Imagine that you are an alien visiting Earth. Your observations have given you an idea of how fast humans grow up: You can see children who are younger and smaller than adults and you can see full-grown, older adults. You haven't visited hospitals to see newborn babies, but you can predict about how big they are based on how large humans are and how fast they can grow.

This is like the way scientists pictured the formation and growth of galaxies before JWST. Then when JWST came along, it was like we were the alien finally getting to visit the hospital. And instead of tiny babies, we found that lots of newborns were actually the size of toddlers! In other words, JWST is showing us that young galaxies are much bigger, brighter, and more numerous than we predicted. For scientists, it's a *very* interesting discovery! Figuring out how the universe quickly created bright galaxies might totally change what we thought about how galaxies form.

Q: WHAT'S YOUR ADVICE FOR SPACE-LOVING KIDS?

A: I've wanted to be an astronomer my entire life. At this playground where I used to play, there was a cement tube that someone had drawn buttons inside, like it was a spaceship. I used to lie in there and pretend to be flying through space. But the first time I told an adult my dream of becoming an astronomer, he laughed at me! Luckily, I didn't listen.

If you have a dream, go after it and don't listen to the naysayers. If you are interested in astronomy, there's a place for you. I work with all kinds of people: Some are scientists, of course, but others are science writers or visual designers. There is always going to be a way to do what you love.

(Above) Images from JWST show that the early universe was filled with far more galaxies than experts expected. There are tens of thousands of galaxies in just the image above.

(Right) An up-close view of galaxy NGC 7496 shows a supermassive black hole at the galaxy's center. It's spewing out massive amounts of energy in the form of jets and winds.

3

WHAT SECRETS
HIDE IN OUR SOLAR SYSTEM?

IF YOU WERE TO VISIT SATURN'S MOON TITAN, IT MIGHT LOOK FAMILIAR.

Like Earth, it has rivers, lakes, and oceans. But they aren't made of water: They're made of liquid methane and ethane—flammable gases on Earth! A future space boat wouldn't need to carry fuel to travel Titan's strange waterways, because it could use the methane and ethane for power (but it *would* need to carry oxygen to burn them!). New images from JWST have revealed that not only do methane and ethane fill Titan's rivers, lakes, and seas, but clouds of the stuff also float in its skies.

What else remains unknown about our planetary neighborhood? Experts are using JWST to find out.

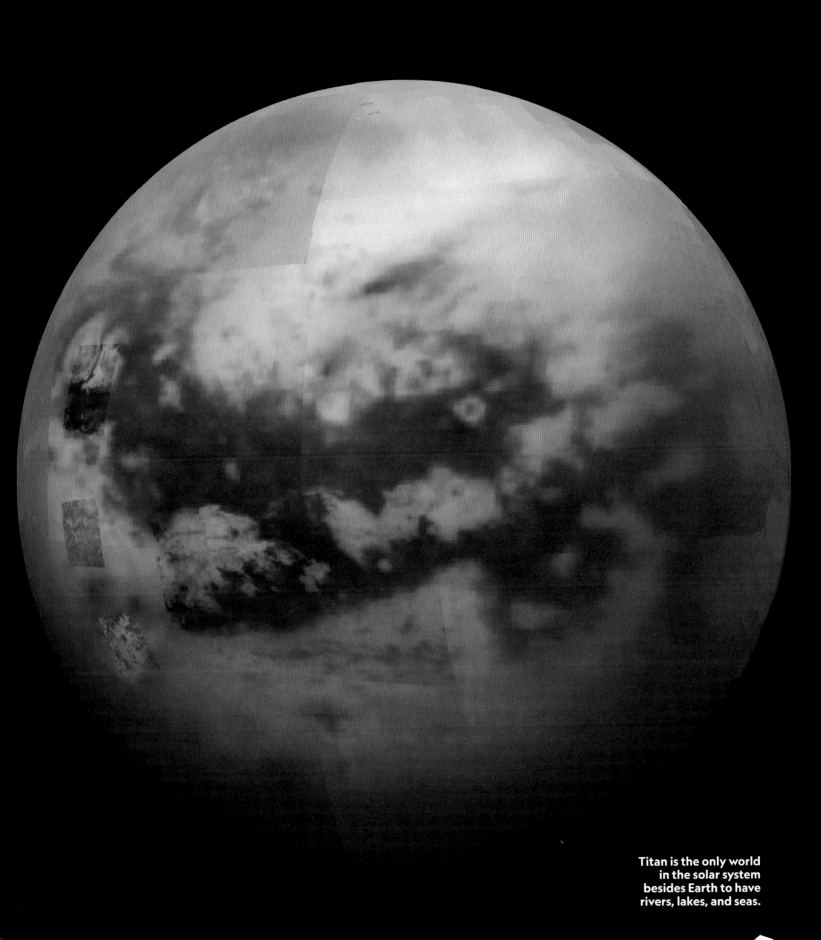

Titan is the only world
in the solar system
besides Earth to have
rivers, lakes, and seas.

BUILDING THE
INFRARED CAMERAS

How do you work a camera when you're standing a million miles away? That's the challenge engineers faced when they set out to create the infrared cameras that allow JWST to look into the distant cosmos.

NEW VIEW

JWST works like an eye: It takes in light from the direction it's facing. JWST's mirror is similar to the pupil of your eye, but enormous in size. As the mirror collects light, it directs that light to JWST's three cameras. The cameras are located within three of its four scientific instruments. Together, the cameras can capture all types of infrared light.

JWST's ability to capture infrared light allows scientists to see all sorts of space stuff in a new way. Not only does infrared allow them to peer at the very oldest stars and galaxies, it also gives them the ability to see straight through dust clouds to discover what's going on inside.

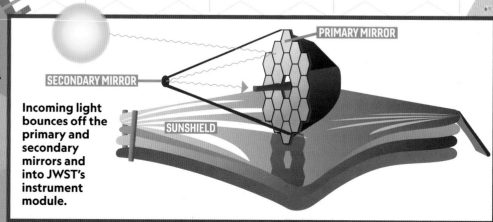

PRIMARY MIRROR

SECONDARY MIRROR

SUNSHIELD

Incoming light bounces off the primary and secondary mirrors and into JWST's instrument module.

WORKING TOGETHER

Building JWST's cameras was a challenge. But the most nerve-racking part was setting them up once the telescope reached outer space—if something went wrong, JWST would be too far away for human hands to fix. First, engineers directed the telescope to remove special parts called snubbers that held each of the 18 mirror segments in place during takeoff. Then they waited for the cameras to cool down enough to start collecting images.

Once the telescope was nice and cold, technicians started adjusting the mirrors' positions to get them perfectly lined up. The telescope would take a test picture, then beam it down to Earth for engineers to study. The engineers would send up instructions that would move each of the mirrors a tiny bit, then take another test picture and move the mirrors again. The painstaking process took three months! But at the end, the mirrors were positioned so perfectly that they now work as one giant mirror.

WORK BEGAN ON THE CAMERAS IN 2002, ALMOST 20 YEARS BEFORE THE TELESCOPE LAUNCHED!

The NIRCam is JWST's main imaging instrument. It is excellent at detecting light from the very youngest stars and galaxies.

TELESCOPE ROUNDUP

JWST is already smashing records. But many of the questions it's answering could never have been asked in the first place without the telescopes that came before it. From the very first simple tube-shaped device that ever swung skyward, to a hunter of alien worlds, these are the telescopes that changed everything.

GALILEO'S TELESCOPE

In 1609, Galileo was the first person to turn a telescope toward the sky and record what he saw. And what he saw shocked him: Everyone had believed the moon was as smooth as a marble, but Galileo saw that it was covered with craters and mountains. He saw the moons of Jupiter and spots on the sun. By watching the motion of these bodies, he realized that it was the sun, not Earth, that was the center of the solar system. Because this went against the Catholic Church's teachings at the time, Galileo was put on trial and spent the rest of his life under house arrest. (Today, we know he was right.)

NEWTON'S TELESCOPE

Galileo's telescopes used a series of lenses, or pieces of curved glass. But there was a limit to their power: They could only make images about 30 times larger. Sixty years after Galileo, Sir Isaac Newton used a new kind of telescope called a reflecting telescope, which was able to see objects that were much farther away by using a curved mirror to gather light instead of a lens. Newton's observations helped him figure out that the same force of gravity that causes an apple to fall from a tree on Earth also pulls the sun, planets, and moons into orbit around one another. This discovery forever changed our understanding of the universe.

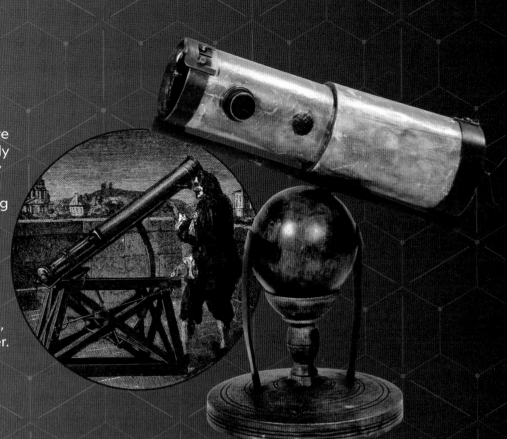

KEPLER

Until the early 1990s, nobody knew for sure whether there were planets outside our solar system, called exoplanets. And there was no telescope dedicated to tracking them down until 2009, when scientists launched the Kepler space telescope. It was a stunning success: Kepler found not only that there are exoplanets all over the universe, but that there are a *lot* of them. In fact, experts now think almost every star in the sky has at least one planet orbiting around it! Scientists also think that it's possible some of those planets could be home to alien life—and one of JWST's missions is to learn more.

HUBBLE

Galileo's telescope allowed us to peek into space, and Newton's used mirrors to gain power. Later telescopes got bigger and better. But they still all shared one problem: From their position on the ground, they had to peer into the sky through Earth's atmosphere. Pockets of moving air cause light to bend as it passes through the atmosphere, which is why stars appear to twinkle. (Stars actually give off steady and constant light, but when that light bends, it looks like twinkling to the human eye.) Enter the first ever space telescope: Hubble, which launched in 1990. From its position above Earth's atmosphere, it has discovered supermassive black holes in the centers of galaxies, uncovered the presence of mysterious dark matter and dark energy, and even revealed the age of the universe.

MEET NAOMI ROWE-GURNEY

Naomi Rowe-Gurney is a planetary scientist using JWST to study Neptune, Uranus, and some of the solar system's moons at the NASA Goddard Space Flight Center in Greenbelt, Maryland, U.S.A.

Q: WHAT MYSTERIES ARE LEFT ABOUT OUR SOLAR SYSTEM?

A: The solar system might sound like old news. But there is a lot left to learn! For example, the giant icy planets Uranus and Neptune are still totally mysterious to us. We haven't visited them since the 1980s, when the Voyager 2 space probe spent just a few days taking photos on its way past these planets. And that's all we have! We don't know why Uranus is the only planet in the solar system that's rotating tipped over on its side. We don't understand why it's colder than Neptune, even though Neptune is farther from the sun. We don't know why Neptune has winds that blow at over 1,200 miles an hour (2,000 km/h), the fastest in the solar system ... especially because this planet is so far from the sun, its source of energy.

Q: ANY CHANCE THERE'S ALIEN LIFE IN OUR OWN SOLAR SYSTEM?

A: Some scientists think our own solar system is the best place to look for life outside of Earth! Both Europa, a moon of Jupiter, and Enceladus, a moon of Saturn, are totally covered with thick ice. But beneath this icy layer, they may have enormous oceans. These oceans might be warmed by heat coming from the inside of the moon. On Earth, we have something similar: vents at the bottom of the ocean that spew out superheated water mixed with chemicals that provide energy for whole communities of strange plants and animals. Europa and Enceladus could have similar environments where living things might also survive.

Both of these moons have plumes of water that erupt from their surfaces, like geysers here on Earth. But because these moons have very low gravity, the water shoots very far—some more than 6,000 miles (10,000 km) into the sky! JWST can use its spectrometers to find out what molecules might be hiding in these water plumes. Scientists will look for what are called biosignatures: evidence of molecules that are created by living things. If they find them, that's a hint that we might share our solar system with alien creatures.

Q: HOW CAN JWST SOLVE THESE MYSTERIES?

A: A lot of my work uses both Hubble and JWST together. A lot of people think that JWST is "taking over" for Hubble, but that's a myth! These telescopes are incredibly powerful when used together. For example, we are using them to take a close look at the dark blue spots on Neptune. Most likely, these are huge storm systems with extremely strong winds, much like Jupiter's Great Red Spot. But unlike the Great Red Spot, they disappear and reappear regularly. The dark spots only appear as visible light, which Hubble can sense. But we can use JWST to peer above and below the clouds of Neptune, at different levels of its atmosphere. That can help us understand what's happening on the planet.

RINGS OF NEPTUNE

SATURN ISN'T THE ONLY PLANET IN THE SOLAR SYSTEM WITH RINGS.

Jupiter, Uranus, and Neptune—the other giant planets—all have them too! JWST gave us one of the clearest images of Neptune's rings ever taken. Neptune's rings are made up of small rocks, gas, and dust. How the planet got them is a mystery that experts are working to uncover. Some think Neptune's rings are some of the youngest rings in the solar system. They could have been formed when one of Neptune's moons got too close to the planet and was torn to pieces by Neptune's gravity.

UNLIKE SATURN'S RINGS, **NEPTUNE'S RINGS ARE INCREDIBLY DARK IN COLOR,** MAKING THEM HARD TO SEE.

MORE MYSTERIES
OF OUR SOLAR SYSTEM

What else will JWST uncover about our own galactic neighborhood? Scientists can't wait to point the most powerful space telescope in history at all kinds of moons, planets, and asteroids. Here are a few of the biggest questions they hope to answer.

DISAPPEARING RINGS

Saturn might be famous for its rings. But someday it won't have them anymore. As Saturn's gravity tugs on the rings, they are being pulled into the planet. Dusty ice particles from the rings rain down on the planet—enough to fill an Olympic-size swimming pool every half hour! How long until the rings are gone for good? Scientists aren't sure, but it could be as soon as 100 million years, a blip on the timescale of the universe.

LIFE ON TITAN

No Earth creature would want to vacation on Saturn's largest moon, Titan: It would roast in the moon's extreme temperatures, choke on its atmosphere, and burn in its lakes of methane and ethane. Yet Titan could host alien life. Scientists believe that beneath its surface, it has an enormous ocean of liquid water—a chemical necessary for all life as we know it. And like Earth, Titan might have tectonic activity—that's the force that moves pieces of a planet's surface around and causes volcanoes to erupt. That could provide energy for the chemical reactions that make life possible. If so, Titan could be home to some kind of living creature.

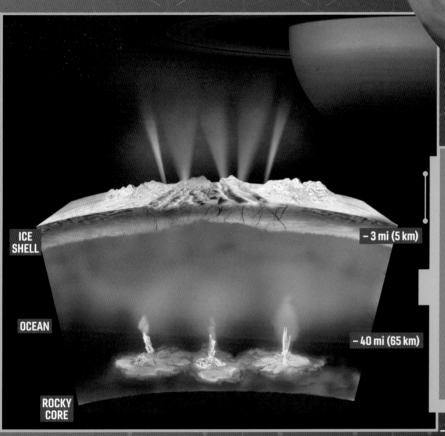

ICE SHELL

OCEAN

ROCKY CORE

– 3 mi (5 km)

– 40 mi (65 km)

WATER WORLDS

Some of the solar system's moons are ocean worlds that spout geysers high into the sky. Others—like our own moon—are dry and dusty places. Why do some moons have lots of water while others have none at all? Scientists know that when a moon is close to its parent planet, the pull of gravity between the two can create the energy needed to keep liquid water on the moon. But some moons—like Saturn's Mimas—are snuggled up close to their parent planet and are still dry as a desert. What gives?

UNKNOWN ZONE

The solar system's most mysterious region is the Kuiper belt. This area is home to tens of thousands of icy objects. It starts beyond the outermost planets and extends out of the solar system into interstellar space. It's dark, far away, and mostly unstudied. Scientists don't even know exactly where it ends, how the icy bodies inside it formed, or whether other star systems have Kuiper belts of their own. JWST will help begin to unravel these mysteries.

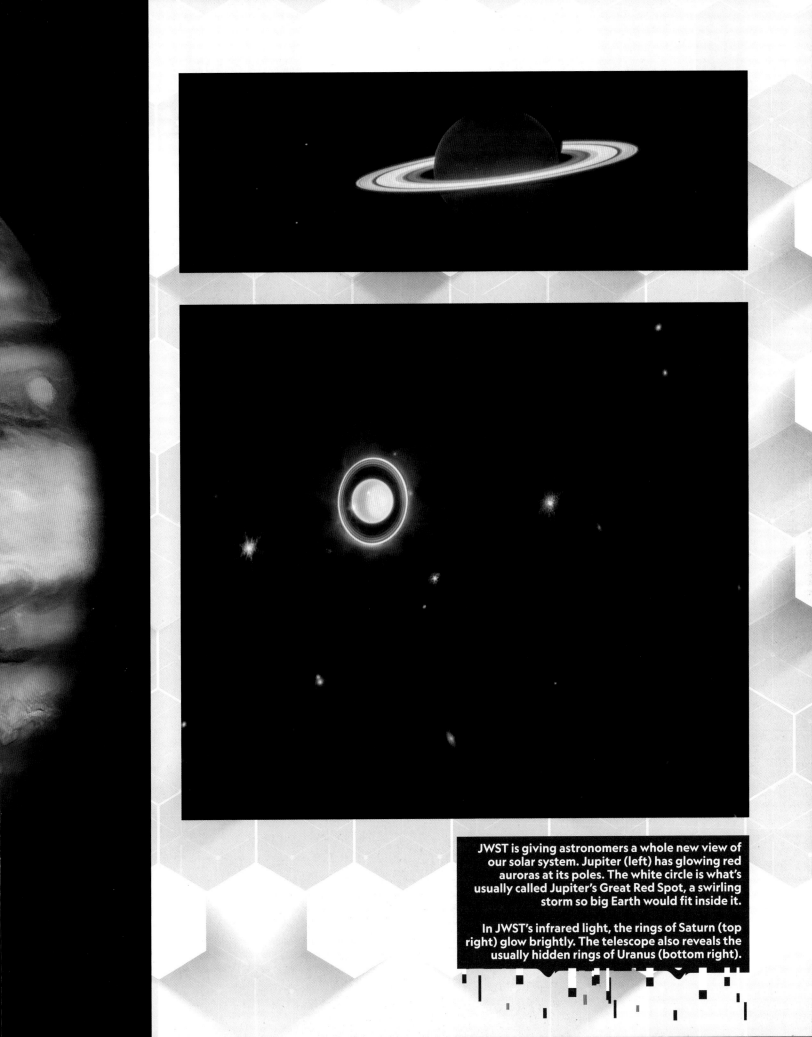

JWST is giving astronomers a whole new view of our solar system. Jupiter (left) has glowing red auroras at its poles. The white circle is what's usually called Jupiter's Great Red Spot, a swirling storm so big Earth would fit inside it.

In JWST's infrared light, the rings of Saturn (top right) glow brightly. The telescope also reveals the usually hidden rings of Uranus (bottom right).

4

HOW ARE STARS BORN?

WATCH STARS AS THEY FORM FOR THE VERY FIRST TIME.

Gas and dust cloud many parts of space, hiding them from the view of most telescopes. But JWST isn't like most telescopes: It has infrared eyes that give it the ability to peer deep into the ancient past. Besides that, it can also look right through that gas and dust to peek at previously hidden places.

This is one of the first JWST images ever released, of an object called the "Cosmic Cliffs" in the Carina Nebula, about 7,500 light-years from Earth. This spot in space is a star nursery, or an area of space where new stars are born. Scientists are using JWST to see stars as they were forming for the very first time. They can also see the very beginnings of planets forming around these new stars, and whether those planets might contain the ingredients of life.

The tallest "peaks" in this image are about seven light-years high: That means it would take seven years to climb them at the speed of light!

BUILDING THE
SPECTROGRAPHS

Have you ever held a prism up to a ray of light? Doing so reveals a secret: Hiding inside every light ray is an entire rainbow of colors. This phenomenon isn't just a party trick. It's also the basis of JWST's most powerful tools.

Instruments called spectrographs aboard JWST look at light coming from objects in space in a whole new way. By studying those images, scientists will be able to solve all kinds of mysteries, including how newborn stars form and move, and whether their planets could contain the ingredients for life.

LIGHT

LIGHT WORK

Light from the sun appears white to our eyes. But it's actually made up of many different colors mixed together. These different colors of light travel at different speeds. When they hit a prism, they bend. Each color bends a different amount, so when the light comes out of the prism, it's all spread out into a rainbow. Red travels the fastest and bends the least, so it appears at the top of a rainbow. Violet, the slowest, bends the most and is always on the bottom.

All types of light are made up of these bands of colors, not just the light that is visible to our human eyes. This includes even the gamma rays produced by exploding stars and the x-rays coming from black holes. JWST's spectrographs can turn this light into rainbow charts called spectra for scientists to study: a type of science called spectroscopy.

SPECTRUM

CARBON

NITROGEN

OXYGEN

IRON

HIDDEN MESSAGES

Different atoms and molecules absorb light in unique ways, creating "fingerprints" in their spectra. By looking for those fingerprints, scientists can learn what a faraway space object is made of. When focusing JWST on a distant nebula, for example, scientists can see if stars form with elements like carbon, oxygen, and nitrogen that might help make their star systems a nice place for living things. Spectra can also reveal temperature, density, and motion. That gives scientists key information about how baby stars behave inside nebulas. And when scientists turn JWST to a faraway planet, spectroscopy can tell them if that planet's skies contain chemicals that, on Earth, are created by living things. That would be a big hint that JWST has discovered alien life.

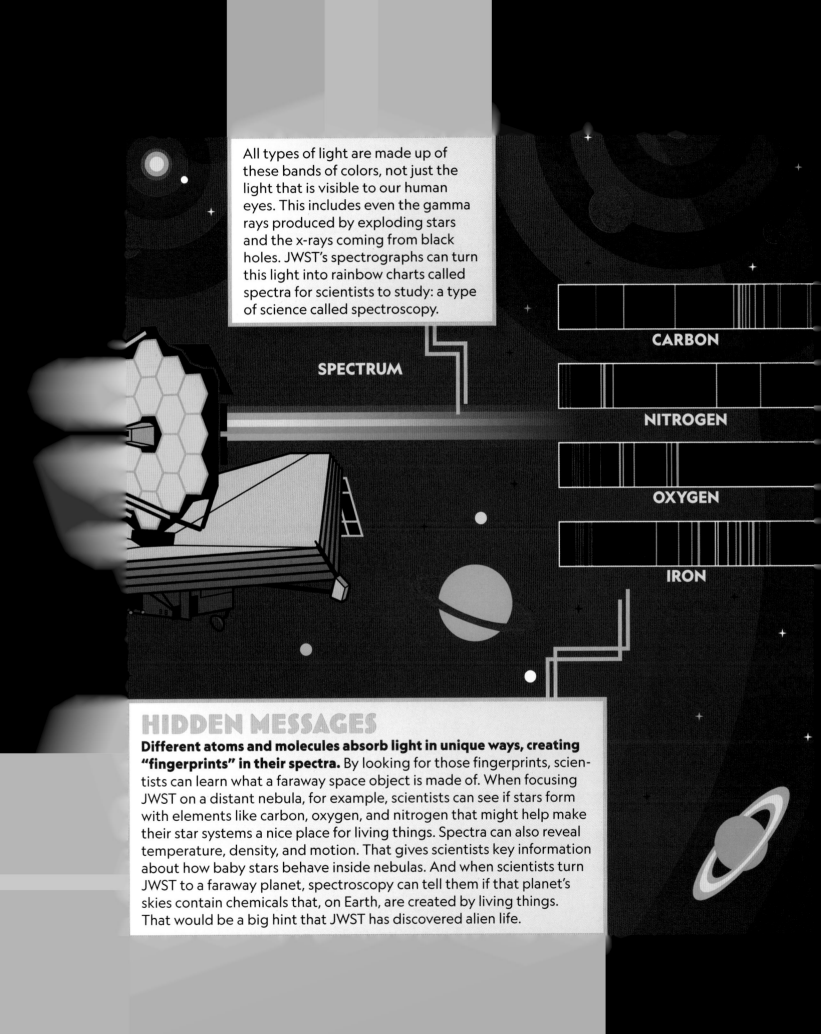

LIFE OF A STAR

Our sun might seem like an unchanging light in our sky. We can count on it greeting us each morning and its heat warming our world. But stars are actually lively objects: They grow old and die, while new stars are constantly being born throughout the universe. Here's how.

A STAR IS BORN

Most stars are born in clouds of gas—mostly hydrogen—and dust. Movement inside these clouds creates areas where gas and dust form dense clumps. When a clump grows massive enough, it starts to collapse under its own gravity.

SHINE BRIGHT

The hydrogen gas that makes up the star's core spins so fast that it heats to 15 million degrees Fahrenheit (8.3 million degrees Celsius). At this extreme temperature, atoms of hydrogen begin to fuse, releasing huge amounts of energy. That's what makes stars shine.

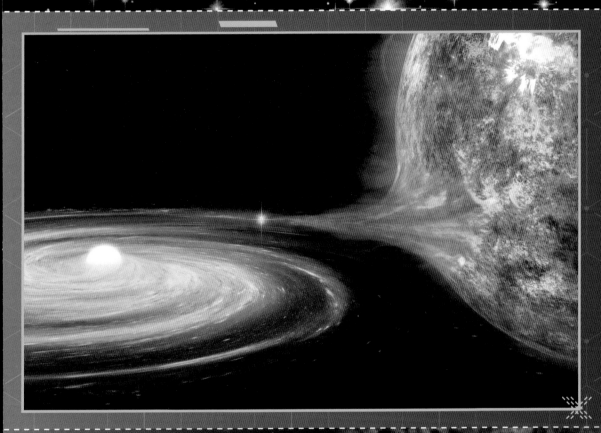

FROM GIANT TO DWARF

Over time, stars run out of hydrogen. Smaller stars, like our sun, puff up into red giants as they throw off their outer layers and their cores cool. Eventually nothing is left but the core: We call this a white dwarf.

GOING SUPERNOVA

Huge stars—say, 10 times the mass of our sun—become supernovas and blow apart in one of the most powerful explosions in the universe. Supernovas can shine brighter than entire galaxies!

MEET MEGAN REITER

Megan Reiter is an astrophysicist using JWST to study the formation of stars at Rice University in Houston, Texas, U.S.A.

Ring Nebula

Q: WHAT'S SOMETHING MOST PEOPLE DON'T REALIZE ABOUT STARS?

A: When very massive stars die, they explode into supernovas. The explosion sets off reactions that can form new elements. Later, these elements can become the building blocks of life. Nearly all the elements in your body, for example, were once made in a dying star. That means we're all made of star stuff!

A: Most of what we know so far is about how individual stars form. But the vast majority of stars in the universe are born in family groups, of sometimes hundreds of thousands of other stars. How do all of these stars interact with each other and with their birthplace? How does that change what we know about how stars form, and how planets form?

JWST is a really powerful telescope. We can use it to look very far away, at very faint stars that we couldn't see well before. JWST is also amazing at looking through gas and dust, which is really important for my work, because stars are born in clouds of gas and dust. If you can see through these clouds, you can see very young stars when they are just starting to put themselves together.

Q: WHAT ARE YOU MOST EXCITED ABOUT?

A: I'm really excited about putting together different pieces of the puzzle of how stars and planets form. This is becoming a bigger and bigger question in astronomy: Does the place where stars are born affect what kind of planets form around them? If we study how stars form in these family groups, we can then figure out which star and planet systems are most likely to get elements from stars nearby. If we understand that, we've gone a long way toward understanding how planets form. That could help us learn which planets are more likely to have the ingredients for life. And that gets us much closer to answering one of the biggest questions of all: Are we alone in the universe?

Spiral galaxy M51

DEATH OF A STAR

JUST BEFORE A HUGE, HOT STAR EXPLODES INTO A SUPERNOVA AND DIES, IT SHEDS ITS OUTER LAYERS.

In March 2023, JWST captured a star called WR 124 in this brief stage, giving scientists an up-close look. WR 124, a star about 30 times more massive than our sun, is located about 15,000 light-years away, in the constellation Sagitta. In this image, it has burned through all its hydrogen—standard star fuel—and has begun fusing atoms of helium instead, a process that whips up extreme winds. These winds are blowing away from the star at millions of miles an hour, carrying the star's outer layers of gas and dust away into space.

THE IRON IN YOUR BLOOD was FORMED IN SUPERNOVA EXPLOSIONS.

BUILDING THE

OOPS!

JWST was designed and built by some of the smartest minds around. But that doesn't mean there weren't hiccups along the way. In fact, the telescope ended up 14 years behind schedule and 20 times over budget! Good thing scientists are used to failure: In fact, it's how they test ideas and ultimately get things right. Here are a few of the biggest obstacles the JWST team had to conquer on their way to scientific success.

SHREDDED

Without its sunshield, JWST would be blind. That's because the shield blocks out light from nearby objects like the sun that would otherwise obscure the telescope's view into deep space. So when engineers discovered that the sunshield had been torn seven times during its assembly, it was a big deal. Onlookers worried that the problem might force NASA to abandon the project. Fortunately, the team was able to fix the problem and keep going.

SHAKEN UP

Blasting off into space is a bumpy ride.
To ensure that JWST would be able to withstand the shaking, engineers built a giant "Vibration Test System," a big table capable of shaking the sensitive instrument up to 100 times per second. When they turned the shake table on, 10 washer nuts came loose. Uh-oh. Technicians fixed the problem, but it added 800 days and $800 million to the project.

NO WAY OUT

In July 2017, JWST began its most important, and most sensitive, test: 100 days in a chamber in Houston, Texas, U.S.A., that simulated the extreme conditions of space. The special chamber was equipped with vacuums to pull out the air and pumps to blast in liquid nitrogen and helium to cool it to temperatures as frigid as those of space. The test was fully under way when something happened that NASA didn't plan for: Record-breaking Hurricane Harvey touched down nearby. Winds howled and water began to fill sidewalks and streets, creeping closer to the $10 billion telescope. Scientists slept in their offices and ate food out of cans, short on supplies and desperate to keep going. A truck filled with precious liquid nitrogen got stuck in the floodwaters. Luckily, the team was able to ride out the storm and complete the test.

STUCK

Scientists put JWST through intense testing
before launch for one reason: If the telescope failed when it was a million miles away, there would be no one around to fix it. So when a gear in one of JWST's infrared instruments got stuck in 2022, after the telescope was in space, it was an astronomy nightmare. JWST had to stop operations while the team analyzed the problem. Fortunately, they were able to come up with a new way to use the instrument that put less stress on the gear, and the telescope returned to its work.

JWST picked up all kinds of star phenomena in the nebula Messier 42 (left), better known as the Orion Nebula, including disks of gas and dust surrounding stars—the beginnings of new star systems.

Sunlike stars are captured in the process of being born in a region of space called Rho Ophiuchi (above).

5

ARE WE ALONE?

THE UNIVERSE IS TEEMING WITH PLANETS.

Outside of our own solar system, all kinds of alien worlds circle faraway suns. Scientists have confirmed the existence of more than 5,000 exoplanets, with nearly 10,000 more that will likely soon be added to the list. Experts now estimate that there could be as many as 100 billion exoplanets in our galaxy alone: It would take more than 9,500 years just to *count* that high.

JWST is giving scientists a new way to look for planets that might have the right conditions to host alien life. One of the very first exoplanets JWST took an image of, named LHS 475 b, is almost exactly the same size as Earth. Like Earth, it's a rocky world. But unlike our planet, it circles its sun at an extreme speed: A year there lasts just two days! Could some strange creatures live on this—or another—faraway world?

LHS 475 b (shown here in an illustration) is only about 41 light-years away: In galactic terms, that's just down the street!

BUILDING THE
CORONAGRAPHS

Imagine you're outside on a warm summer night, trying to spot the glow of a firefly. Now imagine your little brother is shining a huge spotlight right where you're looking. You could never spot a firefly's tiny twinkle in that flood of light! That's exactly the same problem astronomers face when trying to look at exoplanets. Nearly all exoplanets orbit a parent star, which shines so much brighter than the planet that it makes the planet impossible to see ... *nearly* impossible, that is.

HUNTING FOR HINTS

Most of the exoplanets we've spotted weren't found by swinging a telescope around the sky. Instead, these exoplanets were discovered indirectly, using something called the transit method. When a planet passes in front of its much bigger and brighter star, it dims the star's light very slightly. If scientists track a star's brightness for a long time, they will notice regular dips in that light created by a planet orbiting the star.

That might not seem like much information, but experts can tell a surprising amount from tracking transits. By measuring how much the passing planet affects its star's brightness, they can tell how big the planet itself is. From how often the planet completes an orbit, they can estimate its distance from the star. By studying the sunlight that filters through the planet's atmosphere, they can tell what elements are in its skies and even whether the planet's skies are cloudy, hazy, or clear! All this information together can tell them how hot or cold the planet might be—and whether its temperature could be just right for living things.

BEFORE CORONAGRAPHS WERE INVENTED, SCIENTISTS COULD SEE THE SUN'S GREENISH HALO (ITS "CORONA") ONLY DURING A TOTAL SOLAR ECLIPSE.

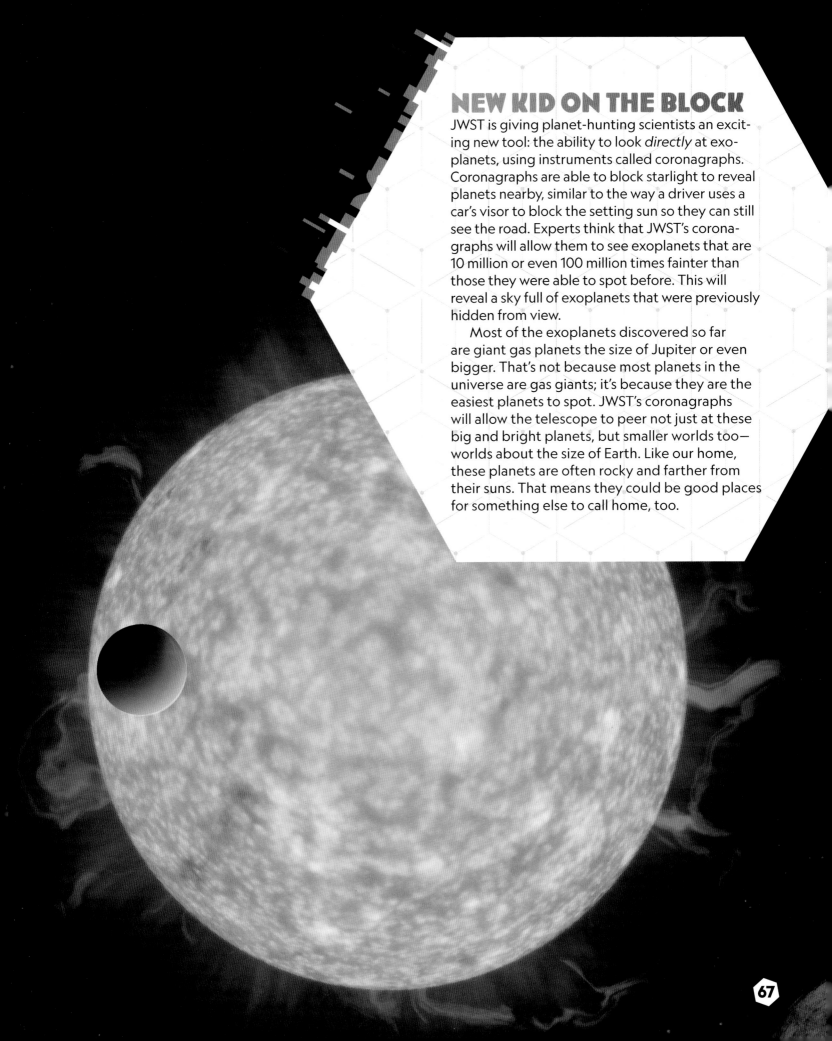

NEW KID ON THE BLOCK

JWST is giving planet-hunting scientists an exciting new tool: the ability to look *directly* at exoplanets, using instruments called coronagraphs. Coronagraphs are able to block starlight to reveal planets nearby, similar to the way a driver uses a car's visor to block the setting sun so they can still see the road. Experts think that JWST's coronagraphs will allow them to see exoplanets that are 10 million or even 100 million times fainter than those they were able to spot before. This will reveal a sky full of exoplanets that were previously hidden from view.

Most of the exoplanets discovered so far are giant gas planets the size of Jupiter or even bigger. That's not because most planets in the universe are gas giants; it's because they are the easiest planets to spot. JWST's coronagraphs will allow the telescope to peer not just at these big and bright planets, but smaller worlds too— worlds about the size of Earth. Like our home, these planets are often rocky and farther from their suns. That means they could be good places for something else to call home, too.

MEET TIFFANY KATARIA

Tiffany Kataria is a planetary scientist who studies the atmospheres and weather of exoplanets at NASA's Jet Propulsion Laboratory in Pasadena, California, U.S.A.

Q: HOW CAN YOU TELL WHAT THE WEATHER IS LIKE ON A PLANET MILLIONS OF MILES AWAY?

GLOBAL TEMPERATURE MAP FOR EXOPLANET HD 189733 B

SUN-FACING LONGITUDE (GRID SPACING: 30°)

A: The first step is understanding what the atmosphere—the gases that surround the planet—is made of. And we can do that using spectrographs like JWST's (see pages 52–53). When we look at a faraway planet, the light we are seeing has traveled through the planet's atmosphere on its way to us. As it goes, it picks up "fingerprints" from molecules within the atmosphere, such as water or methane. JWST's high-tech spectrographs have already given us a wealth of detail about the molecules in many exoplanet atmospheres.

Using infrared telescopes like JWST, we can make heat maps that show what the hottest and coldest regions of the planet are. We can see how the temperature of different parts of the planet changes over time, as the planet orbits its hot star. If you see that the hottest regions of the planet are moving around, that tells you that the planet has wind blowing the heat around. That's the telltale sign of weather.

A: It ties back to how the planets were formed and how they evolved over billions of years. Up until now, we have barely been able to understand anything about the history of these planets. JWST is going to help change that. The molecules in a planet's atmosphere can be linked to the rocks that make up the planet's core, and those rocks are made of stuff left over from stars. By studying the chemistry of exoplanet atmospheres, we can work backward to get a picture of how a planet formed in the first place. That teaches us how our universe came to be.

An illustration of the atmosphere surrounding the gas giant planet WASP-39 b

Q: WHAT'S ONE THING JWST HAS DISCOVERED ABOUT AN EXOPLANET ALREADY?

A: JWST is doing so much that it's hard to keep track of everything that's going on! But one of its first really big, really cool discoveries was about a planet called WASP-39 b. Humans would not survive a visit there: It has extremely fast winds that howl at about 5,000 miles an hour (8,000 km/h). It rains tiny glass particles. And it's hot; I mean really hot—thousands of degrees Fahrenheit!

At those temperatures, all kinds of weird chemistry is going on. And when we looked at WASP-39 b with JWST, we saw that its atmosphere contained something surprising: a gas called sulfur dioxide. This was surprising to scientists because the presence of sulfur dioxide means that a process called photochemistry is taking place. That's where sunlight hitting the planet's atmosphere creates chemical reactions. This is similar to photosynthesis on Earth, how plants make energy from sunlight. Now that we know this molecule exists on WASP-39 b, we will be looking for it on other hot, Jupiter-size planets.

An illustration of a geyser on Europa

TWIN SUNS

IMAGINE WAKING UP EVERY MORNING TO NOT ONE, BUT

TWO SUNS

RISING IN THE SKY.

That's what it's like on exoplanet VHS 1256 b. This planet, about 40 light-years away, is orbiting twin suns, just like the fictional world of Tatooine from *Star Wars*. Scientists have known about VHS 1256 b since 2015. But in 2023, JWST was able to look directly at the planet and measure what its atmosphere is made of. To their surprise, scientists found that the planet's skies are thick with hot, roiling clouds that rain down silicates—similar to grains of sand on Earth. What a wild world!

SEARCH FOR LIFE

For most of human history, people thought Earth was all there was. Then we realized the moon and sun were not just lights in the sky, but other objects in space. In time, we found that we were in a star system of many planets all spinning together. Then we learned that there are other star systems outside ours, too: About 4,000 have been confirmed in just our Milky Way galaxy alone. And there could be as many as two trillion galaxies! With so many places that could host living things, most experts think it's extremely likely that we are not alone in the universe. Here are four potential signs of life JWST is on the lookout for.

BREATHE IN

When planet Earth was young—before the first living things formed in our oceans—its skies were filled mostly with carbon dioxide. But then, the first bacteria and other tiny organisms emerged. They breathed in carbon dioxide and breathed out oxygen. Over millions of years, this transformed Earth's atmosphere into something that insects, birds, and mammals—including humans—could breathe. Detecting oxygen in an exoplanet's skies would be a big hint that something could be living there.

TREES AND OTHER LAND PLANTS PRODUCE ABOUT 30 PERCENT OF EARTH'S OXYGEN.

Amazon rainforest

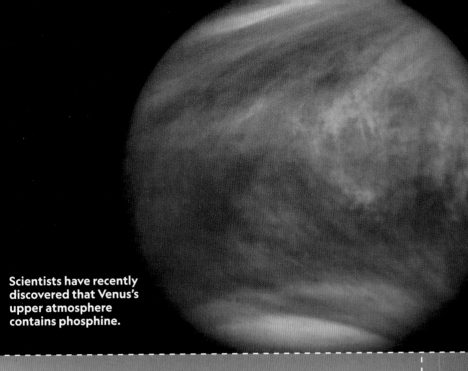

Scientists have recently discovered that Venus's upper atmosphere contains phosphine.

GAS OUT

To humans, phosphine is not a pleasant chemical. It's toxic, explosive, and smells like garlic and rotting fish. It is common on gas giant planets such as Jupiter. But it's also produced on Earth by tiny organisms, including those that live in the guts of animals. That means that its presence on a rocky, Earthlike planet would signal that some kind of life could make its home there. Scientists also look for ammonia, another foul-smelling gas produced by animals on Earth.

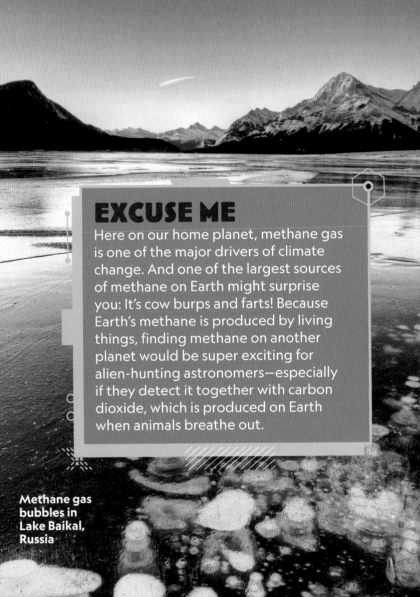

EXCUSE ME

Here on our home planet, methane gas is one of the major drivers of climate change. And one of the largest sources of methane on Earth might surprise you: It's cow burps and farts! Because Earth's methane is produced by living things, finding methane on another planet would be super exciting for alien-hunting astronomers—especially if they detect it together with carbon dioxide, which is produced on Earth when animals breathe out.

Methane gas bubbles in Lake Baikal, Russia

Hot gas planet HD 209458 b

OFF-KILTER ATMOSPHERE

But what if life on another planet looks nothing like life on Earth? What if it doesn't breathe in oxygen and breathe out carbon dioxide or phosphine? Scientists would have no idea what molecules to look for. But they do know to look for something else: an unstable atmosphere. While the skies of lifeless planets like dusty Mars never change, Earth's atmosphere is constantly changing as living things guzzle some chemicals and expel others. An unstable atmosphere would be a clue that a faraway planet might be home to alien creatures.

73

LOOKING
FORWARD

JWST's discoveries are coming so fast it's hard for experts to keep up. As soon as the telescope began operating, its onboard thrusters and wheels started spinning it from spot to spot around the sky. It was looking from star to planet to galaxy, sometimes switching up its target every hour. It can collect more than 50 gigabytes of information each day—that's the equivalent of tens of thousands of books! It will take scientists years to work their way through all that information.

SHAKING THINGS UP

Astronomers can't say exactly what JWST will find out. Humans have barely begun to comprehend so many things the telescope is studying—the birth of stars, the makeup of the early universe, the conditions on distant planets—that it's impossible to predict exactly what we will discover. But that's what makes JWST so exciting. What experts can say for certain is that this telescope is already shaking up what we thought we knew about the universe.

And JWST is just getting started. In just its first two years of operation, enough data has been gathered for 10 years of scientific research. And experts estimate that the telescope has enough fuel to operate for at least 20 years—and perhaps much longer. Scientists expect that JWST will revolutionize astronomy. Its discoveries might make the decades to come the most exciting time in space science, ever.

JWST COULD DETECT **THE HEAT OF A BUMBLEBEE** AS FAR AWAY AS THE MOON.

TELESCOPE OF TOMORROW: EXTREMELY LARGE TELESCOPE

Hubble and JWST broke barriers as space-based telescopes. But the next generation of telescopes will come back down to Earth. One is the Giant Magellan Telescope, so big it will need to be stored inside a 22-story building on top of a mountain in Chile. If all goes to plan, it will be the first of the U.S. Extremely Large Telescope Program, a network of large telescopes around the world opening over the next decade that will work together to solve space mysteries.

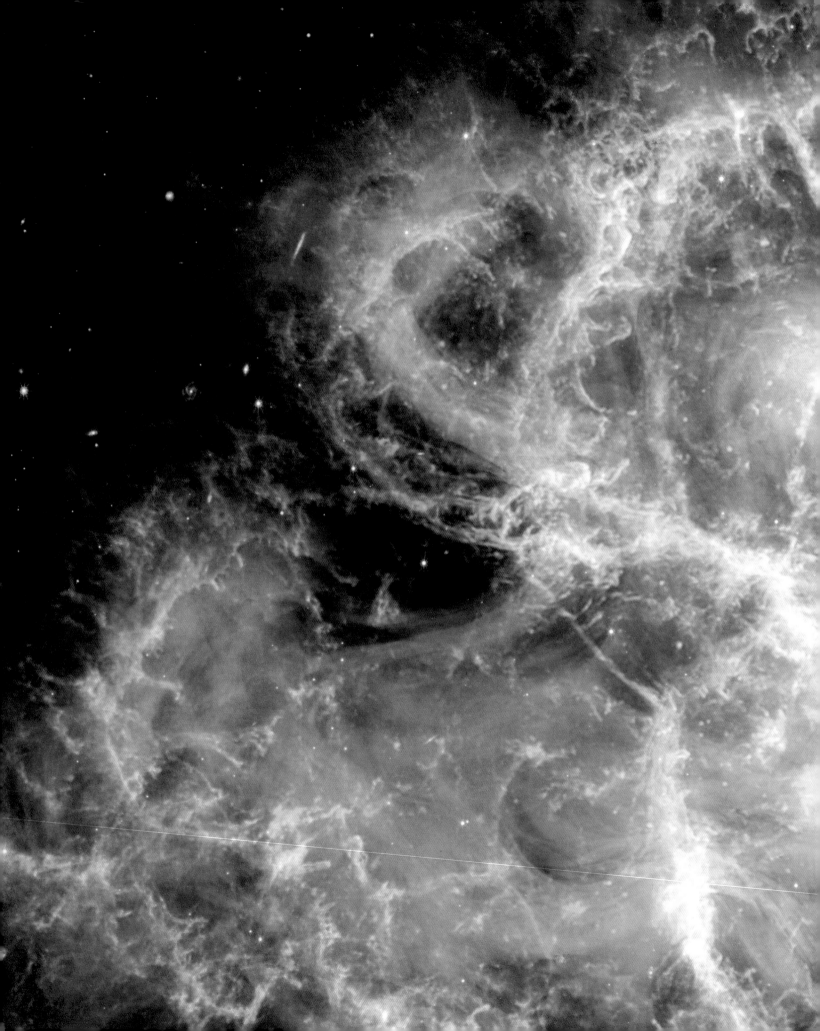

In the year 1054, Chinese, Japanese, Korean, and Arab astronomers wrote of a new star so bright it could be seen during the day. It was actually an exploding star. This JWST image shows the remains of the supernova, located 6,500 light-years away in the constellation Taurus.

INDEX

CREDITS

FRONT COVER: (UP LE), NASA, ESA, CSA, STScI, Webb ERO Production Team; (UP CTR), NASA, ESA, CSA, and STScI; (UP RT), NASA, ESA, CSA, and O. De Marco (Macquarie University), with image processing by J. DePasquale (STScI); (LO LE), Bill Ingalls/NASA; (LO CTR), X-ray: NASA/CXC/Penn State Univ./ L. Townsley et al.; IR: NASA/ESA/CSA/STScI/ JWST ERO Production Team; (LO RT), NASA/ ESA, CSA, and STScI; (inset), NASA/dimazel/ Adobe Stock; (light streaks), HTU/ Shutterstock; (blue hexagons), Yanie/ Shutterstock; (green hexagons), strizh/ Shutterstock; (background hexagons), shuttersv/Shutterstock; **FRONT FLAP:** NASA, ESA, CSA, Image Processing: M. Zamani (ESA/ Webb); (vector frame glitch), Denys Holovatiuk/Shutterstock; **SPINE:** NASA/Chris Gunn; **BACK COVER:** NASA, ESA, CSA, Image Processing: M. Zamani (ESA/Webb); (inset), NASA/dimazel/Adobe Stock; **BACK FLAP:** NASA, ESA, CSA, Image Processing: M. Zamani (ESA/Webb); **THROUGHOUT:** (light streaks), HTU/Shutterstock; (blue hexagons), Yanie/ Shutterstock; (green hexagons), strizh/ Shutterstock; (background hexagons), shuttersv/Shutterstock; (vector frame glitch), Denys Holovatiuk/Shutterstock; **FRONT MATTER:** 1, NASA, ESA, CSA, STScI; 2-3, X-ray: NASA/CXC/Penn State Univ./L. Townsley et al.; IR: NASA/ESA/CSA/STScI/JWST ERO Production Team; 3 (inset), NASA/dimazel/ Adobe Stock; 4-5, NASA, ESA, ESO-Chile, ALMA, NAOJ, NRAO, Image Processing: Alyssa Pagan; 6, ESA/Webb, NASA, CSA, M. Zamani (ESA/Webb), PDRs4ALL ERS Team; 7, ESA/ Webb, NASA, CSA, T. Ray (Dublin); **CHAPTER 1:** 8, Igor Zh./Shutterstock; 9, hooyah808/Adobe Stock; 11, Jude Buffum/Mendola Ltd; 12-13, NASA/Bill Ingalls; 13, NASA/ESA/D. Ducros; 14, NASA, J. Olmsted (STScI); 14-15, NASA; 15, NASA, ESA, CSA, STScI; 16, Jude Buffum/ Mendola Ltd; 16-17, Jude Buffum/Mendola Ltd; 18 (UP), NASA; 18 (CTR), NASA/dimazel/ Adobe Stock; 18 (LO), left image: NASA, ESA, CSA, STScI; right image: NASA, ESA, and The Hubble Heritage Team (STScI/AURA); Acknowledgment: N. Smith (University of California, Berkeley); 19 (UP), ESA/Webb, NASA & CSA, L. Armus, A. Evans; the Hubble Heritage Team (STScI/AURA)-ESA/Hubble Collaboration; 19 (LO), ESA/Webb, NASA & CSA, J. Lee and the PHANGS-JWST and PHANGS-HST Teams; 20 (UP), Ball Aerospace; 20 (LO), Ben Gallagher (Ball Aerospace) and Quantum Coating Incorporated; 21, NASA/ Chris Gunn; **CHAPTER 2:** 22, NASA, ESA, ESO-Chile, ALMA, NAOJ, NRAO, Image Processing: Alyssa Pagan; 23, NASA, ESA, CSA, STScI, Webb ERO Production Team; 25, NASA, ESA, CSA, STScI; 25 (inset UP), NASA, ESA, and the Hubble SM4 ERO Team; 25 (inset LO), NASA,

ESA, and the Hubble SM4 ERO Team; 26-27, NASA/Desiree Stover; 28-29, NASA, ESA, CSA, STScI, Webb ERO Production Team; 30, X-ray: NASA/CXC/Wesleyan Univ./R.Kilgard, et al; Optical: NASA/STScI; 31 (UP), ESA/Hubble & NASA; 31 (LO), X-ray: NASA/CXC/Penn State/G. Garmire; Optical: NASA/ESA/STScI/ M. West; 31 (LO RT), ESA/Hubble & NASA; Acknowledgment: Gilles Chapdelaine; 32 (portrait), Arthur Mount/Mendola Ltd; 32 (UP), NASA, ESA, CSA, K. McQuinn (RU), and A. Pagan (STScI); 32 (LO), NASA/ lukszczepanski/Adobe Stock; 32-33, NASA's Goddard Space Flight Center/CI Lab; Animator, Krystofer Kim (KBRwyle) [Lead], Producer, Scott Wiessinger (KBRwyle) [Lead], Technical support, Aaron E. Lepsch (ADNET); 34, NASA, ESA, CSA, Brant Robertson (UC Santa Cruz), Ben Johnson (Center for Astrophysics, Harvard & Smithsonian), Sandro Tacchella (University of Cambridge, Marcia Rieke (Univ. of Arizona), Daniel Eisenstein (Center for Astrophysics, Harvard & Smithsonian), and Alyssa Pagan (STScI); 35, NASA, ESA, CSA, and J. Lee (NOIRLab), A. Pagan (STScI); **CHAPTER 3:** 36, hideto999/Shutterstock; 37, NASA/JPL/ University of Arizona/University of Idaho; 38, Dana/Adobe Stock; 38-39, Lockheed Martin; 40, Sarin Images/Granger; 40 (inset), SSPL/Science Museum/Getty Images; 41 (UP LE), Science History Images/Alamy Stock Photo; 41 (UP RT), Ann Ronan Picture Library/ Heritage Images/Print Collector/Getty Images; 41 (LO LE), NASA; 41 (LO RT), NASA/Ames/JPL-Caltech/T Pyle; 42 (portrait), Arthur Mount/ Mendola Ltd; 42 (UP), NASA, ESA, CSA, K. McQuinn (RU), and A. Pagan (STScI); 42 (LO), David Aguilar; 43 (UP), David Aguilar; 43 (LO), dottedyeti/Adobe Stock; 44-45, NASA, ESA, CSA, STScI; 46, NASA/JPL-Caltech/Space Science Institute; 47 (UP), NASA/JPL-Caltech/ University of Nantes/University of Arizona; 47 (CTR), NASA/JPL-Caltech/Southwest Research Institute; 47 (LO), Tim Brown/ Science Source; 48, NASA, ESA, CSA, STScI, R. Hueso (University of the Basque Country), I. de Pater (University of California, Berkeley), T. Fouchet (Observatory of Paris), L. Fletcher (University of Leicester), M. Wong (University of California, Berkeley), J. DePasquale (STScI); 49 (UP), NASA, ESA, CSA, STScI, Matt Tiscareno (SETI Institute), Matt Hedman (University of Idaho), Maryame El Moutamid (Cornell University), Mark Showalter (SETI Institute), Leigh Fletcher (University of Leicester), Heidi Hammel (AURA). Image Processing: J. DePasquale (STScI); 49 (LO), NASA, ESA, CSA, STScI, with image processing by Joseph DePasquale (STScI); **CHAPTER 4:** 50-51, Science: Megan Reiter (Rice University); Image: NASA, ESA, CSA, STScI; Image Processing: Joseph DePasquale (STScI),

Anton M. Koekemoer (STScI); 52-53, Jude Buffum/Mendola Ltd; 54, ESA/Hubble & NASA, J. C. Tan (Chalmers University & University of Virginia), R. Fedriani (Chalmers University); Acknowledgment: Judy Schmidt; 55 (UP), NASA, ESA, and T. von Hippel (Embry-Riddle Aeronautical University); Processing: Gladys Kober (NASA/Catholic University of America); 55 (CTR), NASA/CXC/M.Weiss; 55 (LO), NASA, ESA, CSA, STScI and ERO Production Team; 56 (portrait), Arthur Mount/Mendola Ltd; 56 (UP), NASA, ESA, CSA, K. McQuinn (RU), and A. Pagan (STScI); 56 (LO), ESA/Webb, NASA, CSA, M. Barlow (University College London), N. Cox (ACRI-ST), R. Wesson (Cardiff University); 56-57, ESA/ Webb, NASA & CSA, A. Adamo and the FEAST JWST team; 58-59, NASA, ESA, CSA, STScI and ERO Production Team; 60, NASA; 60-61, NASA/Chris Gunn; 62, NASA, ESA, CSA/Science leads and image processing: M. McCaughrean, S. Pearson; 63, NASA, ESA, CSA, STScI, Klaus Pontoppidan (STScI), Image Processing: Alyssa Pagan (STScI); **CHAPTER 5:** 64, NASA, ESA, CSA, STScI, Webb ERO Production Team; 65, Illustration: NASA, ESA, CSA, Leah Hustak (STScI); Science: Kevin B. Stevenson (APL), Jacob A. Lustig-Yaeger (APL), Erin M. May (APL), Guangwei Fu (JHU), Sarah E. Moran (University of Arizona); 67, ESA/ATG medialab/ Science Source; 68 (portrait), Arthur Mount/ Mendola Ltd; 68 (UP), NASA, ESA, CSA, K. McQuinn (RU), and A. Pagan (STScI); 68 (LO), NASA/JPL-Caltech/H. Knutson (Harvard-Smithsonian CfA); 69 (UP), NASA, ESA, CSA, Joseph Olmsted (STScI); 69 (LO), Mark Garlick/Science Photo Library/Alamy Stock Photo; 70-71, NASA, ESA, CSA, Joseph Olmsted (STScI); 72 (UP), vovan/Shutterstock; 72 (LO), Matthew Williams-Ellis/Robert Harding/Adobe Stock; 73 (UP), ISAS, JAXA, Akatsuki; Processing: Meli thev; 73 (LO LE), pictureguy32/Adobe Stock; 73 (LO RT), NASA/ JPL-Caltech/T. Pyle (SSC); 74, Alexandr Mitiuc/ Adobe Stock; 74-75, Giant Magellan Telescope – GMTO Corporation; 75, Giant Magellan Telescope – GMTO Corporation; 76-77, NASA, ESA, CSA, STScI, T. Temim (Princeton University); **BACK MATTER:** 78-79, NASA, ESA, ESO-Chile, ALMA, NAOJ, NRAO, Image Processing: Alyssa Pagan; 80, NASA, ESA, CSA, STScI

Since 1888, the National Geographic Society has funded more than 14,000 research, conservation, education, and storytelling projects around the world. National Geographic Partners distributes a portion of the funds it receives from your purchase to National Geographic Society to support programs including the conservation of animals and their habitats. To learn more, visit natgeo.com/info.

For more information, visit nationalgeographic.com, call 1-877-873-6846, or write to the following address:

National Geographic Partners, LLC
1145 17th Street NW
Washington, DC 20036-4688 U.S.A.

More for kids from National Geographic: natgeokids.com

National Geographic Kids magazine inspires children to explore their world with fun yet educational articles on animals, science, nature, and more. Using fresh storytelling and amazing photography, *Nat Geo Kids* shows kids ages 6 to 14 the fascinating truth about the world—and why they should care. natgeo.com/subscribe

For rights or permissions inquiries, please contact National Geographic Books Subsidiary Rights: bookrights@natgeo.com

Designed by Eva Absher-Schantz, David Marvin (pages 50–55), and Lauren Sciortino (pages 56–61)

Hardcover ISBN: 978-1-4263-7678-8
Reinforced library binding ISBN: 978-1-4263-7699-3

The publisher would like to thank Munazza Alam for providing an expert review and Quyen Hart, Naomi Rowe-Gurney, Megan Reiter, and Tiffany Kataria for contributing interviews to the book. Book team: Katharine Moore, senior editor; Lori Epstein, photo manager; Katherine Kling, fact-checker; and Alix Inchausti, senior production editor.

Printed in China
24/LPC/1